Paul Kegan

Songs for the Year

In Two Parts. Part II - Spring and Summer

Paul Kegan

Songs for the Year
In Two Parts. Part II - Spring and Summer

ISBN/EAN: 9783744664134

Printed in Europe, USA, Canada, Australia, Japan

Cover: Foto ©Thomas Meinert / pixelio.de

More available books at **www.hansebooks.com**

ＳONGS

FOR THE YEAR

PART II.

Spring and Summer

For High Schools, Normal Schools
and Classes

SCOTT, FORESMAN AND COMPANY, PUBLISHERS
378-388 WABASH AVENUE, CHICAGO

SONGS
FOR THE YEAR

IN TWO PARTS

PART II—SPRING AND SUMMER

FOR HIGH SCHOOLS, NORMAL SCHOOLS AND CLASSES

CONTAINING SONGS FOR DECORATION DAY, MAY DAY, EASTER,
DEVOTIONAL AND PATRIOTIC SONGS, AND A FEW OF
THE BEST GLEES AND CHORUSES

SPECIAL PROVISION FOR BASS VOICES

Price, 15 cents

SCOTT, FORESMAN AND COMPANY, PUBLISHERS
378-388 WABASH AVENUE, CHICAGO

TABLE OF CONTENTS.

SONGS OF THE SEASONS.

SONGS OF NATURE.

PATRIOTIC AND HEROIC SONGS.

DEVOTIONAL.

OCCASIONAL.

MISCELLANEOUS.

Songs for the Year

PART II.

SPRING AND SUMMER.

The Contented Heart.

German.   C. G. Neefe.

Moderato.

mf

1. I need not ask for gold or wealth If I con-tent-ed be; If
2. Sweet beau-ty blos-soms for our sake In mead-ow, wood, and vale, And
3. When up the sun in splen-dor goes All ra-diant shines the earth And
4. And then I sing my song of praise, My heart grows full of love, My

mf

God but grant me strength and health It is e-nough for me. I'll
birds their sweet-est songs a-wake And tell their vary-ing tale. The
splen-did in her jew-els glows, A bride of roy-al worth. I
voice in pray'r I fain would raise To One who dwells a-bove. And

sing with thankful heart and strong At morn and eve a joy-ful song.
trill-ing lark at morn-ing light, The coo-ing night-in-gale at night.
needs must think this beau-ty rare Was giv'n, that we its joy might share.
ev-er thankful will I be To Him who giv-eth all to me.

Hush-a-by, Baby.

F. L. Lorraine. Arranged.

Andante.

Hush - a - by, ba - by, On the tree top,

When the wind blows the cra - dle will rock, When the bough bends the

cra - dle will l, And down comes ba - by, cra - dle and all.

A Song of Praise.

Translated from the German.

Gruenberger.

Andante.

1. Thou has built the glo-rious mountain, Shaped the riv-er's might-y bed,
2. Thou dost lead the flight of swal-lows, Thou dost show the stars their way;
3. All Thy creat-ures, Lord most ho - ly, Praise Thy name for ev - er - more.

Raised the hap-py, leap - ing fountain, Made the flee - cy clouds o'er-head,
Sea - son af - ter sea - son fol-lows; Thou didst or - der night and day.
All Thy works, both high and low-ly, Tell Thy pow'r, Thy love a - dore.

The King in Thule.

Translated from Goethe.

K. F. Zelter.

1. An an - cient king in Thu - le Was faith - ful to the grave, To
2. The gift he fond - ly treas-ured, He quaffed it at each feast, And
3. And when his end was near - ing, His heir each cas - tle old He
4. With - in his lord - ly pal - ace, His pal - ace by the sea, He
5. Then rose the an - cient mon - arch, He drank the cup's red glow, Then
6. He saw it fill - ing, sink - ing, Deep sink - ing in the sea; His

whom his dy - ing la - dy A gold - en gob - let gave.............
tears they rose and gath - ered Be - fore the draught had ceased............
gave, with hoard - ed treas - ure, All save the cup of gold..............
sat with knights and vas - sals At feast and rev - el - ry................
cast the sa - cred. beek - er In - to the flood be - low...............
eyes in death were clos - ing, And ne'er a - gain drank he..............

A Study.

Pursuit.

Wm. Rowley.
From 17th Century Lyrics.

W. W. Gilchrist.

Tempo di valse.
grazioso

1. Art thou gone in haste? I'll not for - sake thee;
2. All a - long the plain, To the low foun - tains,

Tempo di valse.

Runn'st thou ne'er so fast, I'll o'er - take thee:
Up and down a - gain From the high moun - tains;

O'er the dales, o'er the downs, Thro' the green mead - ows,
Ech - o then shall a - gain Tell her I fol - - low,

From the fields thro' the towns To the dim shad - ows.
And the floods to the woods Car - ry my hol - la!

mf
Hol - la, Ho! hol - la, Ho! Hol - la, Ho! Ho!
Ho! Ho!................. Hol - la, Ho! Ho!.......

f
Hol - la, Ho! hol - la, Ho! Ho! Ho! Ho!
Ho! Ho! Ho! Ho! Ho!

Land of Greatness, Home of Glory.

(Austrian National Hymn.)

A. J. Foxwell.

Haydn.

1ST AND 2ND SOPRANO.

Andante.

1. Land of great-ness, home of glo - ry, Might-y birth-place of the free,
2. No - ble deeds of old in - spir-ing Ev - 'ry heart with lof - ty aim,
3. Homes by safe de - fence sur - rounded, Rights which made our free - dom sure,

ALTO—TENOR.

TENOR AND BASS.

Famed a - like in song and sto - ry, All thy sons shall hon - or thee,
Now our em - u - la - tion fir - ing, Lead us on to great - er fame.
Laws on e - qual jus - tice found-ed, These will loy - al - ty se - cure.

North and South are firm - ly band-ed, East and West as one u - nite;
So shall love and truth un - shak-en, Stur - dy cour - age, hon - est worth,
While with love and zeal un - ceas-ing, We are join - ing heart and hand,

All   by   hon - or   well   com - mand-ed,   Strong   in   striv-ing   for   the   right.
Might - y   ech - oes   still   a - wak- en   To   the   far - thest bounds of   earth.
Shine,   in   brightness   yet   in - creas-ing,   Shine,   O   dear - est   Fa - ther-land.

Welcome, Wild Northeaster!

Charles Kingsley.

George Jaspersen.

Allegro.

1. Wel-come, wild North-east - er! Shame it   is   to   see   Odes to   ev - 'ry
2. Tired we are of sum - mer, Tired of gaud - y   glare,   Show - ers   soft and

Melody in the bass.

zeph - yr, Ne'er   a   verse   to thee. Welcome, black Northeast-er,   O'er the   Ger-man
stream - ing Hot   and breathless air.   Tired of list-less dream-ing Thro' the   la - zy

foam,   O'er the   Dan - ish   moorlands, From thy   froz - en   home.
day;   Jov - ial   wind of   win - ter   Turn us   out   to   play.

My Native Land.

Andante.   Wohlfahrt.

1. Faith-ful lov-ing, no-bly prov-ing, This I swear with heart and hand, All I
2. Brings to-mor-row joy or sor-row, Still, my heart will con-stant be; Country

Andante.

mf

am, and all I may be, It is thine, my fa-ther-land. Not a-
mine, with bonds e-ter-nal All thy sons are knit to thee. Faith-ful

lone in tune-ful meas-ure Will I praise thee while I live; For thy
lov-ing, no-bly prov-ing, This I swear with heart and hand, All I

free - dom, dearest treasure, Gladly I my life would give.
am, and all I may be, It is thine, my fa - ther - land.

mf

Kelvin Grove.

Con spirito.

Scotch.

p

p

1. Let us haste to Kel - vin Grove, bon - ny las - sie, O; Thro' its
2. We will wan - der by the mill, bon - ny las - sie, O; To the
3. Ah! I soon must bid a - dieu, bon - ny las - sie, O; To this
4. And when on a dis - tant shore, bon - ny las - sie, O; Should I

cresc.

mf

ma - zes let us rove, bon-ny las - sie, O; Where the rose in all its pride Paints the
cot be - side the rill, bon-ny las - sie, O; Where the glens rebound the call Of the
fair - y scene and you, bon-ny las - sie, O; To the streamlet winding clear, To the
fall 'midst battle's roar, bon-ny las - sie, O; Wilt thou, fair - est, when you hear Of thy

mf   *cresc.*

dim.   *p*

hol - low din - gle side, Where the midnight fair - ies glide, bon - ny las - sie O.
loft - y wa - ter fall, Thro' the mountain's rock-y hall, bon - ny las - sie O.
fra - grant scented brier, And to thee of all most dear, bon - ny las - sie O.
lov - er on his bier, To his mem - 'ry drop a tear, bon - ny las - sie O?

dim.   *p*

A Storm.

Bryan Waller Proctor.

W. W. Gilchrist.

Vivace.

1. The spir-its of the might-y sea To-night are wak-en'd from their dreams And

up-ward to the tem-pest flee, Bar-ing their fore-heads in the gleams; The

light'nings run and thun-ders cry, Rush-ing and rain-ing thro' the sky.

Be-hold, trem-bling bil-lows head-long go,

2. Be-hold, like mil-lions massed in bat-tle, The trem-bling bil-lows

head-long go, And dash, and dash in

head-long go, Dash-ing the bar-ren deeps which rat-tle In

mist - y tem - pest till they grow, And burst,

mist - y tem - pest till they grow All fruit - ful in their

and burst and burst from fren - zy in - to foam.

rock - y home and burst from fren - zy in - to foam.

The Falcon.

J. R. Lowell.
Andante.

A. Conradi.

1. I know a fal - con swift and peer - less As e'er was cra - dled
2. No harm - less dove, no bird that sing - eth Shud-ders to see him
3. Let fraud and wrong and base - ness shiv - er, For still be - tween them

in the pine; No bird had ev - er eye so fear - less Or -
o - ver - head; The rush of his fierce swoop-ing bring - eth To
and the sky The fal - con Truth hangs poised for - ev - er And

wing so strong as this of mine, Or wing so strong as this of mine.
no - no-cent hearts no thrill of dread, To in - no-cent hearts no thrill of dread.
marks them with his venge-ful eye, And marks them with his venge-ful eye.

Come Unto These Yellow Sands.

From "The Tempest."

Henry Purcell.
arr. by John Hullah.

Come un - to these yel - - - - low sands And

there take hands, Come un - to these yel - - - - low sands And there take hands; Foot it feat - ly here and there, And let the rest the

bur-then bear, Foot it feat · ly here and there, And let the rest the bur-then bear.

CHORUS.

Hark! hark! the watch dogs bark; Hark! hark! I hear..... the

Come Unto These Yellow Sands.

strain of chan-ti-cleer, Hark! hark! I hear...... the strain of chan-ti-cleer.

rall. molto la 2da volta

Twilight at Sea.

Amelia B. Welby.
By per. of Ford, Howard & Hulbert.

Folksong.

p. Andante.

The twi - light hours, like birds, flew by, As light - ly and as free, Ten

thous - and stars were in the sky, Ten thous - and on the sea; For

ev - 'ry wave with dim - pled face That leaped up - on the air, Had caught a star in

its em - brace, And held it trem-bling there, And held it trem-bling there.

Maynard.

Welsh.

Moderato.

mf

1. Spring-time is re-turn-ing, The win-ter cold and gray, With snow and nip-ping
   Birds sing in the branch-es Where bud-ding leaves are seen, And ev-'ry dus-ky
2. Soft-ly blows the south-wind A-long the hills and dales While mer-ri-ly brooks
   Flocks now leave the moun-tains, To browse a-round the fields, And crop the dain-ty

mf

dim.

frost will soon have pass'd a-way; } Now no more a-far is heard the hunter's winding horn,
hedge is tint-ed o'er with green. }
flow thro' all the sun-ny vales; } Soon will maidens in the bow-ers seek the vio-lets pale,
herb-age coming springtide yields. }

dim.

p

And with care the farm-er guards his fields at ear-ly morn, } Spring-time is re-
Soon the hawthorn white with blos-som will per-fume the gale; }

cresc. *cresc.* *dim.*

turn-ing; the winter cold and gray, With snow and nipping frost will soon have pass'd a-way.

cresc. *cresc.* *dim.*

Spring Song.

Translated from the German.

M. Vogel.

1st SOPRANO.

Andante.

mf

1. Birds are singing, flow'rs are blooming, Spring's bright flags are all un-furled.
2. Joy we'll meet in ev-'ry path-way, She doth sing with ev - 'ry bird,

2nd SOPRANO.

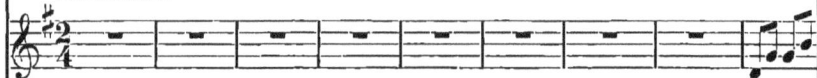

1. Birds are
2. Joy we'll

Andantino.

p   *p*

cresc.   *f*   *dim.*

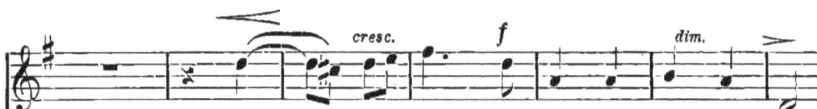

Spring's bright flags are all, are all un - furled.
She doth sing with ev - 'ry, ev - 'ry bird,

cresc.   *f*

sing - ing, flow'rs are bloom - ing, Spring's bright flags are all un - furled.
meet in ev - 'ry path - way, She doth sing with ev - 'ry bird.

cresc.   *f*   *dim.*

animato.

Come, oh, come then, let us wan-der, Thro' the sha-dy wood-land yon-der
Soft in flow-er-heart she's bed-ded, Hid in grass with dew be-thread-ed

mf

animato.

p *cresc.* *f* *dim.*

Far in God's wide sun-ny world, Far in God's wide sun-ny world.
Murm-'ring where a stream-let's heard, Murm-'ring where a stream-let's heard.

p *cresc.* *f* *dim.*

p *cresc.* *sf marcato* *sf* *sf* *dim.*

20

Morning Song.

Celia Thaxter.

W. W. Gilchrist.

Grazioso.

1. We launch our boat ...... up-on the
fade our child - hood's shores. With-
with our hope .. the un-known

spark - ling sea, ... We dip our rhyth - mic oars with song and
out re - gret. .... We leave the safe, green, hap - py fields, and
fu - ture gleams, ... Freighted with cliss - ful dreams our barque floats

cheer; .... Be - fore our danc - - ing prow the
try .... The vague, un - cer - - tain o - cean,
on, ... And life a shin - - ing path of

shad-ows flee,........ Be-hind us fast the fair coasts dis - ap - pear.
storm be - set; .... Nor see the tem-pests that be - fore us lie.
vic - t'ry seems, ... Crown'd with a gold - en peace when day is done.

1, 2.   **3.**

2. So
3. Flush'd

ppp

Praise Ye the Lord.

Isac Watts.   Wohlfahrt.
Maestoso.

mf

1.   Praise ye the Lord,'tis good to raise Our hearts and voi - ces in His praise;
2.   Great is the Lord, and great His might, And all His glo - ries in - fin - ite;
3.   He loves the meek, re - wards the just, The wick - ed hum - bles in the dust,

mf
cresc.

His na - ture and His works in - vite To make this du - ty our de - light.
His wis - dom vast, and knows no bound, A deep where all our tho'ts are drowned.
Melts and sub - dues the stub-born soul, And makes the bro - ken spir - it whole.

cresc.

MY OLD KENTUCKY HOME, GOOD-NIGHT.

Moderato.
dolce

Stephen C. Foster.

1. The sun shines bright in the old Ken-tuck - y home, 'Tis
2. They hunt no more for the pos - sum and the coon On the
3. The head must bow and the back will have to bend Wher-

dolce

sum - mer, the dark - ies are gay, The corn - top's ripe and the
mead-ow, the hill, and the shore; They sing no more by the
ev - er the dark - y may go; A few more days, and the

mead - ow's in the bloom, While the birds make mu-sic all the day; The
glim - mer of the moon On the bench by the old cab - in door; The
trou - ble all will end In the field where the su - gar canes grow; A

young folks roll on the lit - tle cab - in floor, All
day goes by like a shad - ow o'er the heart, With
few more days for to tote the wea - ry load. No

mer - ry, all hap - py and bright; By'n - by Hard Times comes a-
sor - row where all was de - light; The time has come when tho
mat - ter, 'twill nev - er be light, A few more days till we

knock - ing at the door; Then, my old Ken-tuck - y home, good-night!
dark - ies have to part; Then, my old Ken-tuck - y home, good-night!
tot - ter on the road; Then, my old Ken-tuck - y home, good-night!

CHORUS.

mf

Weep no more, my lady, Oh! weep no more to-day; We will sing one song for the

old Ken-tuck - y home, For the old Ken-tuck - y home far a - way.

The Spring Journey.

R. Heber.
Moderato.

L. Spohr.

mf

1. Oh, green was the corn as I rode on my way, And bright were the
2. The thrush from his hol - ly, the lark from his cloud, Their cho - rus of
3. The mild south-ern breeze brought a show'r from the hill, And yet tho' it
4. Oh, such be life's jour - ney, and such be our skill, To lose in its

mf

dews on the blos - soms of May, And dark was the syc - a - more's
rap - ture sang jov - ial and loud From the soft ver - nal sky to the
left me all drip - ping and chill, I felt a new pleas - ure as
bless - ings a sense of its ills; Through sun - shine and show'r may our

leaf to be - hold And the oak's ten - der leaf was of em - 'rald and
soft grass - y ground, There was beau - ty be - neath me, a - bove, and a -
on - ward I sped, To gaze where the rain - bow gleamed broad o - ver-
pro - gress be e - ven And our tears lend a charm to the pros-pect of

gold, And the oak's ten - der leaf was of em - 'rald and gold.
round, There was beau - ty be - neath me, a - bove, and a - round.
head, To gaze where the rain - bow gleamed broad o - ver - head.
heav'n, And our tears lend a charm to the pros - pect of heav'n.

From the German.

F. L. Schubert.

Andante marcato.

mf

1. 'Neath Spring's glad heav'n, thro' Au - tumn rain, In Summer's pleasure, in Win - ter's pain,
2. Where still in sunshine the greenwoods lie, 'Mid trees high-tow'ring to reach the sky,

mf

3. A - far in God's wide world to rove, As free as flies each fleet-winged dove,
4. They wan - der gai - ly till comes the night, Then dance and sing in the moon's soft light;

mf

Gyp - sies roam ev'rywhere, Blithesome and free from care. La, la, la, la,
Like deer, in bosk-y dell Gyp-sies de - light to dwell.

This is the gypsies' joy, Pleas. ure with-out al - loy. La, la, la, la, la, la,
Then in a grass-y nest Each hap-py soul doth rest.

la, la, la, la, la, la, la, la, la, la, la, la, la.

la, la, la, la, la, la, la, lu, la, la, la, la, la, la, la, la, la, la.

The Snow Melts Fast.

Hoelty.

W. W. Gilchrist.

1. The snow.................. melts fast, May comes.............. at last.
2. Who can.................... fore - tell The toll - - ing bell

Allegro.

1. The snow....... melts fast, May comes..... at last, Now
2. Who can......... fore - tell The toll - - ing bell When

shoots each spray Forth blos-soms gay, The war - bling bird A - round is heard, A -
we with May No more shall play? Canst thou fore - tell The com - ing knell, The

Come, twine................ a wreath, And on.................. the heath
Re - joice,................ re-joice, So spake.............. His voice

round is heard, Come, twine....... a wreath, And on........... the heath
com - ing knell? Re - joice,....... re-joice, So spake......... His voice

cresc.

The dance pre - pare, Ye maid - ens fair, The dance pre - pare, Ye maid - ens fair,
Who gave us birth For joy on earth, Who gave us birth For joy on earth;

Dance on the heath.
En - joy its prime.

Come, twine a wreath, Dance on the heath, Dance on the heath.
God gives us time, En - joy its prime, En - joy its prime.

Translated from the German.

R. Schalm.

1. The sum - mer days are com - ing, For drow - sy bees are
2. When sum - mer days are com - ing, The time has come for

hum - ming, Spring's mild - er days, with sun and rain, Have waked the fields of
roam - ing. Then let us haste in field and lea To greet her, full of

ten - der grain, And pret - ty flow'rs a - bloom-ing, The gen - tle air per-
mirth and glee, Who brings the crim - son ro - ses, Who Na - ture's wealth dis-

fum - ing, And voice of bird pro-claims That sum-mer's com - ing.
clos - es, With bird and bee re - joice, For sum-mer's com - ing.

Mark the Merry Elves.

Callcott.

Allegretto.

Mark the mer-ry elves of fair - y land, Mark the mer -ry elves of fair - y

Mark the mer-ry elves of fair - y land, Mark the mer-ry elves of fair - y

land, In the cold moon's gleam-y glance, In the cold moon's gleam-y

land, In the cold moon's gleam-y glance, In the cold moon's gleam-y

glance, In the cold moon's gleamy glance

glance, In the cold moon's gleamy glance They with shad-ow - y mor-rice dance,

They with shad-ow - y mor -rice dance.

They with shad-ow - y mor -rice dance. Soft mu - sic dies a-

Soft mu - sic dies a - long the des - ert

pp   *p*
Soft mu-sic dies a-long the des-ert land, a-

long the land, Soft mu - sic dies, Soft mu-sic dies a-long tho des-ert land, a-
dim.
laud,.................................... Soft mu - sic dies a-

Adagio.
dim.   *cresc.*   *Spiritoso.*
long the des - ert land.   a-long the des-ert land. Soon,at peep of cool-cy'd
dim.   *cresc.*
long the des - ert land.   a-long the des-ert land. Soon,at peep of cool-cy'd
dim.   *cresc.*

dim.   *Spiritoso.*
day, Soon the num-'rous lights de-cay, Soon,at peep of cool-ey'd day, Soon the
dim.
day, Soon the num-'rous lights de-cay, Soon,at peep of cool-ey'd day, Soon the
dim.

rall.   *Tempo primo.*
num-'rous lights de - cay. Mer-ri-ly, now mer-ri-ly, mer-ri-ly, now mer-ri-ly
rall.
num-'rous lights de - cay. Mer-ri-ly, now mer-ri-ly, mer-ri-ly, now mer-ri-ly
rall.

Mark the Merry Elves.

Aft - er the dew - y moon they fly, Mer - ri - ly, now mer-ri - ly, mer -ri - ly, now

Aft - er the dew - y moon they fly, Mer - ri - ly, now mer-ri - ly, mer -ri - ly, now

mer - ri - ly After the dew - y moon they fly, Aft - er the dew - y moon they

mer - ri - ly After the dew - y moon they fly, Aft - er the dew - y moon they

fly, Mer - ri - ly, now mer - ri - ly, mer - ri - ly, now mer - ri - ly Aft - er the

fly, Mer - ri - ly, now mer - ri - ly, mer - ri - ly, now mer - ri - ly Aft - er the

dew - y moon they fly,....... Aft - er the dew - y moon they fly, they fly, they fly.

dew - y moon they fly,....... Aft - er the dew - y moon they fly, they fly, they fly.

they fly, they fly,

Welcome to Spring.

Bartholomew-Voss.

Allegro vivace.

Mendelssohn.

mf

1. We
2. We

Allegro vivace.

hail thee and wel-come thee, beau - ti - ful May; The heav - ens are az - ure, the
hail thee and wel-come thee, beau - ti - ful Spring, The birds in the for - est all

cresc.

mead-ows are gay; Thou crown - est the bow - ers With verdure and el - e - gant
mer - ri - ly sing, The zeph - yrs are sigh - ing, The bees to their flow-ers are

cresc.

f *mf*

flow - - ers; We hail thee and wel-come thee, beau - ti - ful May; The
lie - - ing; We hail thee and wel-come thee, beau - ti - ful Spring; The

f *dim.* *p*

Welcome to Spring.

heav-ens are az - ure, the mead-ows are gay, Thou crown - est the bow - ers With
birds in the for - est all mer - ri - ly sing; The zeph - yrs are sigh - ing; The

ver - dure and el - e - gant flow - - ers. Thy glit - ter-ing beam Lights
bees to their flow-ers are hie - - ing. The strings of the lute, The

fountain and stream; In-spired by thy glance, They tin-kle and dance: We
breath of the flute, Ac-cord with the lays We sing to thy praise: We

hail..................

thee and wel-come thee, beau - ti - ful May; The
thee and wel-come thee, beau - ti - ful Spring; The

heav-ens are az - ure, the mead - ows are gay; Beau - ti - ful May,
birds in the for - est all mer - ri - ly sing; O beau - ti - ful Spring,

beau - ti - ful May, we wel - come thee!... We hail thee, we hail thee and
beau - ti - ful Spring, we wel - come thee!... We hail thee, we hail thee and

wel - come thee! thee!

Ped.

Full Fathom Five.

SOLO AND CHORUS.

Shakespeare.

Purcell.

Moderato.

SOPRANO.

Full fath - om five thy fa - ther

lies, full fath - om

five thy fa - ther lies, Of his bones is cor - - - al made, Those are pearls that were his eyes; Noth - - ing..... of him that doth

fade,   fade, But doth suf - fer, doth suf - fer a sea - -

change In - to some - thing rich and strange, But doth suf - fer, doth suf - fer a

sea - - change In - to some - thing rich..... and strange.

Full Fathom Five.

Sea nymphs hour - ly ring his knell; Hark! now I hear them,

Sea nymphs hour - ly ring his knell; Hark! now I hear them,

Sea nymphs hour - ly ring his knell; Hark! now I hear them,

coll' 8va

ding dong, ding dong bell,... hark! now I hear them, ding dong, ding dong bell,

ding dong bell, hark! now I hear them, ding dong bell.

ding dong bell,... hark! now I hear them, ding dong bell.

coll' 8va

Hark! now I hear them, hark! now I hear them, hark! now I hear them,

Hark! now I hear them, hark! now I hear them, hark! now I hear them,

Hark! now I hear them, hark! now I hear them, hark! now I hear them,

coll' 8va

ding dong bell, ding, ding dong bell, ding dong bell.

ding dong bell, ding, ding dong bell, ding, ding dong bell.

ding dong bell, ding, ding dong bell, ding, ding dong bell.

coll' 8va

Boating Song.

E. I. H.

Edwin G. Monk.

1. The sun is high in heav-en, Yet fresh the zeph-yrs play; The
2. Now lou-ger still, and strong-er, Our Cap-tain strains his oar; The

riv - er gleams be - fore us, Why sit........ we still to - day?
slug-gards well may won - der, Who loll........ up - on the shore.

mf   *f*

Doff daint - i - ness and   pride,.... And
The bark flies down the   riv - er;   A

mf

Doff coat so prim, Doff daint - i - ness and pride,.... And
And fast - er still The bark flies down the riv - er; A

coat so prim and neck - cloth, Doff daint - i - ness and pride,.... And
fast - er still and fast - - er The bark flies down the riv - er; A

coat so prim and neck - cloth, Doff daint - i - ness and pride,.... And
fast - er still and fast - - er The bark flies down the riv - er; A

f

launch our boat so shape - ly Up - on the sil - ver tide,.........
cheer to show our pluck, my boys, It's now as stout as ev - er.

launch our boat so shape - ly Up - on the sil - ver tide,.........
cheer to show our pluck, my boys, It's now as stout as ev - er.

launch our boat so shape - ly Up - on the sil - ver tide,......... And
cheer to show our pluck, my boys, It's now as stout as ev - er. A

launch our boat so shape - ly Up - on the sil - ver, sil - ver tide,
cheer to show our pluck, my boys, It's now as stout, as stout as ev - er.

Boating Song.

And launch our boat Up-on the sil-ver-tide...... } Singing
Our pluck, my boys, It's now as stout as ev-er! }

And launch our boat Up-on the sil-ver-tide...... } Singing
Our pluck, my boys, It's now as stout as ev-er! }

launch our boat,.................. Up - on the sil - ver tide...... } Singing
cheer to show our pluck, my boys, It's now as stout as ev-er! }

And launch our boat Up-on the sil-ver tide...... } Singing
Our pluck, my boys, It's now as stout as ev-er! }

ev - er as so heart-i-ly our ash-en oars we feath-er, With a

ev - er as so heart-i-ly our ash-en oars we feath-er, With a

ev - er as so heart-i-ly our ash-en oars we feath-er, With a

ev - er as so heart-i-ly our ash-en oars we feath-er, With a long pull, and a strong pull, and a pull al - to - geth - er, With a

long pull, and a strong pull, and a pull al - to - geth - er, With a

long pull, and a strong pull, and a pull al - to - geth - er, With a

long pull, and a strong pull, and a pull al - to - geth - er, With a

long pull, and a strong pull, and a pull al - to - geth - er.

long pull, and a strong pull, and a pull al - to - geth - er.

long pull, and a strong pull, and a pull al - to - geth - er.

long pull, and a strong pull, and a pull al - to - geth - er.

42

Now the Bright Morning Star.

John Milton.

Robert Greville.

mf Allegretto.

Now the bright morn - ing star, day's har - bin - ger, Comes dan - -

mf

Now the bright morn - ing star, day's har - bin - ger, Comes

- - cing, comes dan - - - cing, comes dan - cing from the

dan - cing, comes dan - cing, comes dan - cing from the

p east, comes dan cing from the east, *f* Now the bright morn - ing star, day's

f Now the bright morn - ing star, day's

p east, comes dan - cing from the east, Now the bright morn - ing star, day's

p har - bin - ger, Comes dan - - cing, comes dan - - cing, comes *f*

har - bin - ger, *p* Comes dan - cing, comes dan - cing, comes *f*

har - bin - ger, *p* Comes dan - cing, comes dan - cing, comes yel-low, yel-low cow-slip and the pale prim-rose,.... the pale prim-

yel-low, yel-low cow-slip and the pale prim-rose, the pale prim-

rose............

rose,.... She from her green lap throws the yel-low, yel-low

rose............

the yel - - - low

cow - slip and the pale prim - rose, the yel - low

The

The

cow - slip and the pale prim - rose,.... She from.... her green lap

cow - slip and the pale prim - rose,.... She from her green lap

Now the Bright Morning Star.

dan - cing from the east, comes dan - cing from the east, And leads... with

dan - cing from the east, comes dan - cing from the east, And

her, and leads.. with her, and leads with her the flow - - 'ry

leads...with her, and leads....with her the flow - - 'ry May, the flow-'ry

leads with her, and leads with her the flow-'ry May, the flow - 'ry

May,... And leads.... with her...... the flow - - 'ry May,... And leads....with

May,... And leads with her the flow - 'ry May, And leads with

May,...

her..... the

her the flow - 'ry May.... May.... Who from her green lap throws the

her the flow-'ry May.... May.... Who from her green lap throws the

yel - low cow - slip, the yel - low cow - slip,
throws, She from..... her green lap throws, She
throws the yel - low cow - slip and the pale prim-rose, She
throws, She from..... her green lap throws, She
the yel - low cow - slip, the
from her green lap throws, She from her green lap
from her green lap throws, She from her green lap
yel - low cow - slip, the yel - low cow - slip
throws the yel - low cow - slip, the
throws the yel - low cow - slip and the pale prim - rose, the
and the pale prim - rose,.... the pale prim - rose.
cresc.
dim.
p
D.C.
cow - slip and the pale prim - rose,.... the pale prim - rose.
cow - slip and the pale prim - rose,.... the pale prim - rose.
and the pale prim - rose,.... the pale prim - rose.

Marseillaise.

Maestoso.

1. Ye sons of Free-dom, wake to glo - ry, Hark! hark! what myr-iads bid you
2. Oh! lib - er - ty! can man re - sign thee, Once hav - ing felt thy glo - rious

rise; Your children, wives, and grand-sires hoar - y, Be-hold their tears, and hear their
flame? Can ty - rants' bolts and bars con - fine thee, And thus thy no - ble spir - it

cries, Be - hold their tears, and hear their cries. Shall law - less ty - rants, mis - chief
tame, And thus thy no - ble spir - it tame. Too long our coun-try wept, be-

breeding, With hire-ling host, a ruf - fian band, Af - fright and des - o - late the
wail-ing The blood-stain'd sword our conq'rors wield; But free-dom is our sword and

land, While peace and lib - er - ty lie bleeding? }
shield, And all their arts are un - a - vail-ing. }   To arms! to arms! ye brave, The

Marseillaise.

pa - - triot sword un - sheath; March on, march on,

all hearts re - solv'd On lib - - er - ty or death.

Night Fall.

Andante. dolce — Methfessel.

p

1. When the songs of birds are still, And the flow-ers go to rest;
2. In the ev-'ning's gath-'ring shades Oth-er stars, like an-gels' eyes,

mf

When the lone-some whip-poor-will Steals at twi-light from his nest:
Shine from heav'n as day-light fades; Soon in flash-ing bands they rise,

mf

p

Then a star comes o'er the hill Thro' the pale light of the west.
And a mil-lion gold-en maids Bring the mis-tress of the skies.

p

A Wish.

Frederick Manley.

Arranged from L. F. Ritter.

1. As leaf - lets that rus - tle peace - ful - ly When soft - ly the
2. As o - dors that rise from hid - den flow'rs, En - rich - ing the

south wind is blow - ing, As song-birds that soar me - lo - di - ous-
breez-es of spring - time; As shad - ows that dream in twi - light

ly When o - ver the hill - tops dawn is show-ing; So may all your
hours, As light on the mead - ows sleeps at noon-time; So may your last

days be   wealth - y   In   joys that are pure and   health - y.
hour be   peace - ful,   As   in - no - cent and re - pos - ful.

Summer Days.

Moderato.   Eleanor Smith.

1. Sum - mer's sun - ny   days have come; Soft and sweet the   wind   is   blow - ing;
2. Hear   how sweet the   riv - er sings, Ev - er rip-pling,   ev - er   flow - ing;
3. All   the wood is   filled with sound, Sweet the per-fumed air   is   ring - ing,

Bees a - cross the   mead-ows hum, Where the gold - en   flow'rs   are grow - ing;
Tell - ing of a   thousand things, Whence it comes and   with - er   go - ing;
Up   and down and   round and round, Blithesome songs the   birds   are sing - ing,

Fields and trees   are green and   fair,   Sun - shine's sleep - ing   ev - 'ry-where.
Sing - ing like   the birds and   bees   Of   the   won - drous world   it sees.
Oh, the hap - py sum - mer   hours,   When the world's a   world of flow'rs!

A Song.
(EVENING.)

Dieffenbach.

Tranquillo.

Sweet May.

Celia Thaxter.
By permission of Houghton, Mifflin & Co.

C. A. Kern.

Allegretto.

1. Oh! the fra-grance of the air With the breathing of the flow'rs!
2. Oh! the mel-low dip of oars Thro' the dream-y aft-er-noon!

mf *dim.*

Oh! the isles of cloud-lets fair, Shin-ing aft-er balm-y show'rs!
Oh! the waves that clasp the shores, Chanting one de-li-cious tune!

mf

Oh! the fresh-ly rip-pling notes! Oh! the war-bling, loud and long,
Wears the warm, en-chant-ed day To the last of its rich hours,

From a thousand gold-en throats! Oh! the southwind's ten-der song!
While my heart, in the sweet May, Buds and blos-soms with the flow'rs.

Easter Anthem.

Louise Dew.

Henry Carey.

Allegro.

mf *f*

mf *f*

1. Ring, glad joy-bells, ring, oh! ring,   Al - - le - lu - ia,
2. Sing, blithe song-birds sing, oh! sing,   Al - - le - lu - ia,
3. Sing, ye peo-ple, sing, oh! sing,   Al - - le - lu - ia,

mf *f*

mf *f*

mf *f*

Now pro-claim the ris - en King,   Al - le - lu - ia,
Now pro-claim the birth of Spring;   Al - le - lu - ia,
Now pro-claim glad Eas-ter's King.   Al - le - lu - ia,

mf *f*

mf *f*

mf *f*

Who to earth once more re - stores,   Al - le - lu - ia,
Shout for joy, ye trees and hills,   Al - le - lu - ia,
Fra-grant lil - ies, peace im - part,   Al - le - iu - ia,

mf *f*

mf *f*

mf *f*

E - den with wide o - pen doors.   Al - le - lu - ia.
Cloud-less skies, and laugh-ing rills.   Al - le - lu - ia.
Com-fort bear to each sad heart.   Al - le - lu - ia.

mf *f*

Easter Ode.

Frederick Manley.

Eleanor Smith.

Allegretto giocoso.

mf

1. There's a mu - sic up in the froz - en hills Of a ma - ny voi - ced
2. A spir - it hath come to the sleep - ing earth, She hath soft - ly kissed the
3. A - rise, O ye laugh-ter of low - land leas, For your woodland sisters are

Allegretto giocoso.

mf

har - mo - ny; It ris - es and falls with a thousand trills, And all the field with a
life-less snow With radiant lips and hath giv - en birth To souls of streams and their
now a-wake; The spir - it hath kissed the a-nem-o - nes And scattered the light and the

glad - ness fills, And fountains and riv-ers and brooks and rills, Are
gur - gling mirth, Her wings have hung o - ver the plac-es of dearth Till they
bells of the peas, And the chick-weed's stars a - mong the trees And the

p

cresc.

laugh - ing a - loud, ye are free, ye are free! A - rise!............ A -
bud - ded and blos-somed with life in the glow; The light,........... The
vi - o - let blows in the brake, in the brake; The spring,.......... The

cresc.

rit.

rise from your darksome bed and see That winter and death have passed and ye Are
light of her eyes hath pierced be-low The cells of the ice, and bud - lets grow, And
spring has come and in her wake She hath brought the heav'ns to pond and lake— A-

a tempo 1st and 2nd v.   *a tempo 3rd v.*

free, O flow'rs are free!
sap to heav'n doth flow.
wake, O flow'rs, a - - - - - - - wake!

a tempo.   *a tempo.*

54

George Howland.

Decoration Day.

Flemish Folksong.

Andantino.
p dolce.

1. { Ten - der - ly bring - ing our flo - ral ob - la - tion, Strew we the
   { Free - ly their lives for the life of the na - tion, Gal - lant - ly

2. { Scorn - ing their coun - try's true birth - right to bar - ter, Life in the
   { Wor - thi - er, shrine than the grave of the mar - tyr, Free - dom seeks

3. { Where o'er their dust nev - er foe - man shall tri - umph, Safe in earth's
   { Leav - ing be - hind them a death - less ex - am - ple; Peace - ful - ly

p dolce.

graves of the dear ones who gave
dy - ing the death of the brave.
bal - ance they grudg'd not to lay.
not where her hom - age to pay.
bo - som en - fold - ed they rest,
sleep they the sleep of the blest.

mf

Hal - lowed the ground where the
Faith in the right, at no
Let us, then, true to their

mf

loved ones are sleeping, Sa - cred the hour when a - bove them we tread, While in our
dan - ger to fal - ter, Pre - cious in - her - it - ance thus to be - queath; Where finds re -
mem - o - ries meet - ing, Rich in the free - dom they died to make ours, O - ver their

dim.

p

hearts their sweet mem - o - ries keep - ing, Come we to hon - or the glo - ri - ous dead.
li - gion a ho - li - er al - tar Than the green graves, with her garlands to wreathe?
graves while their vir - tues re - peat - ing, Ten - der - ly, lov - ing - ly strew them with flow'rs!

Flowers for the Brave.

E. W. Chapman.

By permission of Harper Bros.

Tschirch.

Moderato.

1. Once a - gain the flow'rs we ga - ther On these sa - cred mounds to lay; O'er the tombs of fall - en he - roes Float the stars and stripes to. day; From the mountain, hill, and val - ley Is - sued forth a no - ble throng, With he - ro - ic val - or fight - ing Till was heard the vic - tor's song, Till was heard the vic - tor's song.

2. But these brave men now are sleep - ing, While their deeds in mem - 'ry live, And the trib - ute we are bring - ing 'Tis the na - tion's joy to give. Bring bright flow'rs the graves to gar - land, Let the sweet - est mu - sic rise, Let the stars and stripes be - wav - ing O'er their gen - 'rous sac - ri - fice, O'er their gen - 'rous sac - ri - fice.

The Lord is My Shepherd.

James Montgomery.   J. Reading.

1. The Lord is my shep - herd, no want shall I know;   I
2. Let good - ness and mer - cy, my boun - ti - ful God,   Still

feed in green pas - tures, safe fold - ed   I rest; He lead - eth   my soul where the
fol - low my steps till I meet Thee a - bove;   I seek   by   the path which my

still   wa - ters flow,...... Re - stores   me when wan - d'ring, re -
fore - fa - thers trod,...... Thro' the land   of their so - journ, Thy

deems when op - press'd   Re - stores me when wand'ring, redeems when oppress'd.
king - dom of love,   Thro' the land   of their so - journ, Thy king-dom of love.

Lead, Kindly Light.

Newman.

Andante.

Dykes.

1. Lead, kind-ly Light, a-mid th'en-cir-cling gloom, Lead Thou me
2. I was not ev-er thus, nor pray'd that Thou Shouldst lead me
3. So long Thy pow'r has blest me, sure it still Will lead me

on; The night is dark, and I am far from home, Lead Thou me
on; I loved to choose and see my path but now Lead Thou me
on O'er moor and fen, o'er crag and tor-rent till The night is

on; Keep Thou my feet; I do not ask to see..........
on; I loved the gar-ish day; and, spite of fears,..........
gone, And with the morn those an-gel fa-ces smile..........

The dis-tant scene, one step e-nough for me.
Pride ruled my will: re-mem-ber not past years.
Which I have loved long since, and lost a-while.

Come, Oh! Come, in Pious Lays.

G. Wither.
Allegro.

J. Stainer.

1. Come, oh! come, in pi - ous lays   Sound we God Al - might - y's praise;
2. Let those things which do not live,   In still mu - sic prais - es give;
3. Come, ye sons of hu - man race,   In this cho - rus take your place,

Hith - er bring in one con - sent   Heart and voice and in - stru - ment;
Low - ly pipe, ye worms that creep   On the earth or in the deep;
And, a - mid the mor - tal throng, Be you mas - ters of the song;

Mu - sic add of ev - 'ry kind,   Sound the trump, the cor - net wind,
Loud a - loft your voic - es strain,   Beasts and mon - sters of the main;
An - gels and su - per - nal pow'rs,   Be the no - blest ten - or yours,

cresc.

Strike the vi - ol, sound the lute;   Let no tongue or string be mute,
Birds, your warb - ling tre - ble sing;   Clouds, your peals of thun - der ring;
Let in praise of God the sound   Run a nev - er - end - ing round;

mf

cresc.

Nor a crea - ture dumb be found That hath ei - ther voice or sound.
Sun and moon, ex - alt - ed higher, And bright stars, aug - ment the choir.
That our song of praise may be Ev - er - last - ing, e'en as He. A - men.

ff

Guide Me, O Thou Great Jehovah.

Wm. Williams.

Flotow.

Moderato.

1. Guide me, O Thou great Jo - ho - vah, Pil-grim thro' this bar - ren land; I am
2. O - pen Thou the crys - tal foun-tain Whence the healing streams do flow, Let the
3. When I tread the verge of Jor - dan, Bid the swell-ing stream subside; Death of

weak, but Thou art might-y; Hold me with Thy power-ful hand. Bread of heav - en,
fier - y, cloud-y pil - lar Lead me all my jour - ney through; Strong De-liv - 'rer,
death, and fell de-struc-tion Land me safe on Ca-naan's side; Songs of prais - es,

Bread of heav - en, Feed me till I want no more; Bread of heav - en, Bread of
Strong De - liv - 'rer, Be Thou still my strength and shield; Strong De-liv-'rer, Strong De-
Songs of prais - es I will ev - er give to Thee; Songs of prais - es, Songs of

heav - en, Feed me till I want no more, Feed me till I want no more.
liv - 'rer, Be Thou still my strength and shield, Be Thou still my strength and shield.
prais - es, I will ev - er give to Thee, I will ev - er give to Thee.

mf

The Sea.

J. Brahms.

1. Zephyrs all are
2. All, all is

sleep - ing, calm is o - cean's breast, Dark'ning shad - ows of eve - ning bid the
still up-on the wave - lets' crest, And my wea - ry heart would fain be

wea - ry rest; Lu-na with a cloudy veil, made of sheerest lace,........
lulled.... to rest; On life's broad o - cean, cradled in the foam,.......

Sails... a - way to dreamland, hides her beam - ing face.
Where the stormy winds revel till my barque sails home.

pp

barque sails home, Where the storm - y winds rev - el till my barque sails

pp

ppp poco rit.

home.

p

62

June.

Rose Terry.
Allegretto.

Danish Tune.

1. Airs of sum-mer that soft-ly blow, Sing your whisp-er-ing
2. Curl the wave on the sun-ny sand, Rock the bee in its
3. Kiss the snows on the moun-tain height, Vex the riv-er that

songs to me, O - ver the grass like a
rose a - sleep, Scat - ter o - dors from
leaps be - neath, Sing in the fir - trees your

shad - ow go, Flut-ter your wings in the nest-ling tree.
strand to strand, O - ver o-cean in laugh-ter sweep.
sweet good night, And cease like a ba - by's slum-b'ring breath.

A Study.

Rebecca B. Foresman.   Ludwig Liebe.

1. 'Tis sum-mer, glad sum-mer; Come, lay your books a-side, And haste to na-ture's
2. 'Tis sum-mer, glad sum-mer; In yon-der clo-ver field A buzz-ing u-ni-
3. 'Tis sum-mer, glad sum-mer, And na-ture o-pens wide Her books, and if you

sum-mer school In mead-ow green and for-est cool Where hap-py birds teach
ver-si-ty, Whose teach-er is a big brown bee, Is dai-ly giv-ing
wish to know How flow-ers bloom and wil-lows grow, While hap-py birds are

sing-ing; In-deed none can sur-pass This glo-rious sing-ing class.
les-sons To those who wish to know How clo-ver blos-soms grow.
sing-ing, Then come to na-ture's school In shad-owy for-ests cool.

Ti-ro

Ti-ro-li,   ti-ro-la,   ti-ro-li,   ti-ro-la,

li,........ ti-ro-la,........ ti-ro-li,........ ti-ro-la,   ti-ro-

ti-ro-li,   ti-ro-la,   ti-ro-li,   ti-ro-li,   ti-ro-la.

li,........ ti-ro-la,........ ti-ro-li,   ti-ro-li,   ti-ro-la.

INDEX.

www.ingramcontent.com/pod-product-compliance
Lightning Source LLC
Chambersburg PA
CBHW021534270326

41930CB00008B/1249